THE INVENTORS
ingenious ideas
creative designs

VELOCIPEDES / BICYCLES

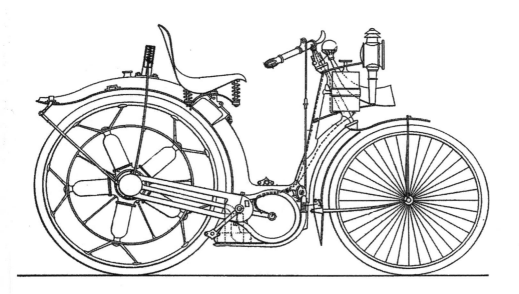

bad burro
PRESS

Bad Burro Press
an imprint of Catalyst Publications, Inc.

The Inventors -- creative ideas ingenious designs – VELOCIPEDES / BICYCLES

Source: United States Patent and Trademark Office, www.uspto.gov

Published by:

Bad Burro Press, an imprint of
Catalyst Publications, Inc.
PO Box 2485, Kirkland, WA 98083-2485

catalystpublicationsinc.com

Printed in the United States of America
First Printing 2016

ISBN 978-1-943783-01-4

TABLE OF CONTENTS

Ingenuity

*The quality of being clever, original, and inventive.
Derived from the Latin term: ingenuitā, innate virtue or freeborn characteristic.*

Each inventor cited in this publication reflects these characteristics. Regardless if the individual applications were successfully manufactured or reaped financial reward, each evidences dedication, determination and creativity.

Patent applications have a long and storied history in the United States. The earliest patent was reportedly granted in Massachusetts to Samuel Winslow in 1641 for a process of making salt. The United States Patent Act of 1790 was founded upon Article 1, Section 8 of the Constitution signed three years earlier: "The Congress shall have Power ... To promote the Progress of Science and useful Arts, by securing for limited Times to Authors and Inventors the exclusive Right to their respective Writings and Discoveries."

According to the United States Patent and Trademarks Office (USPTO), three invention patents were granted in 1790 and thirty-three the following year. The volume increased: 158 in 1808, 24,656 in 1900, 157,494 in 2000 and 300,678 in 2014. Creative genius flourishes, and not just within resident citizens. The first record of USTPO patents granted to foreign residents was in 1836 with 8. That number had risen to 167,000 by 2014.

Inventor statements have been excerpted and drawings specially adapted for this publication. I hope you enjoy this presentation of ingenuity and creativity.

Christopher J. Fox

1. VELOCIPEDES

BIG MONEY IN BICYCLES

It is estimated that there are in America 4,000,000 bicycle riders who have invested $300,000,000 in wheels, $1,000,000 in bicycle clothing and $200,000 in sundries and repairs.

Two hundred and fifty bicycle manufacturers, five large tire makers and 500 manufacturers of sundries, having a total investment of $69,000,000 have benefited by this traffic. The estimated capital invested in retail establishes, repair shops, race tracks and club houses is $21,000,000 making the total American investment in cycling equal to $600,000,000.

During 1896, it is claimed, 1,000,000 wheels and 3,000,000 tires will be produced, giving employment to 75,000 bicycle works and 3,000 tire employees. Fifty thousand persons are employed in sundries factories and 22,000 as retail dealers and repair men, making the total number of persons connected with the bicycle industry 4,250,000.

The Evening Bulletin, Feb. 7, 1897
Maysville, KY.

Value of $1 in 1897 = $27.48 in 2015

Mrs. C. -- "Now, Claude, I know what you were going to say. You were going to tell me that you must desert me every night for six weeks while you learn to ride a velocipede. If wives had their way they'd bury every velocipede in town. And what was the matter with you last night? I couldn't get a wink of sleep. Your legs kept going up and down all night, like pumphandles. Velocipede motion, was it? Put your feet in the stirrups, and turn and throw your knees up and down, does it? Now, don't tell me it's nothing when you get used to it, because that's something Iwon't get used to. It is bad enough to sleep with a man when he is quiet, but to have the bed clothes floping up and down all night as regularly as that clock ticks, is a little too much, velocipede or no velocipede. If you ride that velocipede another day, Claude, I'll leave the house."

Press and Daily Dakotaian, May 07, 1889
Yankton, Dakota Territory [S.D.])

"**MY** invention relates to an improvement in **velocipedes**, the object being to make provision for causing the wheel of the inner and smaller circle described by the velocipede to be authmatically disengaged from the crank-shaft as the **guide-wheel** is turned, and thereby permit the velocipede to be readily turned without undue friction or strain on the wheels or crankshaft, the wheel of the inner and smaller circle as an idler, while the

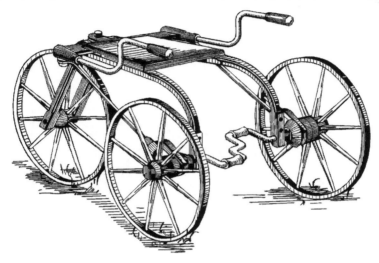

wheel on the outer or larger circle is locked fast to the craskshaft, thereby serving as the propelling-wheel in describing a circle.

By moving the handles laterally in either direction the rider may turn the guide-wheel either to the right or left, and thus turn the velocipede in any desired direction or curve."

United States Patent 231,609
Inventor: PERKINS, NAHUM S.C.
Filing Date: August 24, 1880

At the city council meeting last night, the regular business was transacted, and an ordinance of interest to the wheeling public was passed.

"No person shall ride or propel any bicycle, tandem or velocipede on any of the sidewalks of this city, at a faster rate than five miles per hour, nor be permitted to ride two or more abreast on said sidewalks, nor be allowed to ride after dark on said sidewalks without a lighted lamp in front of said bicycle, tandem or velocipeded. Any person violating this ordinance shall, on conviction, be punished by a fine in any sum not to exceed $25, or by imprinment in the city jail not to exceed 25 days, for each offense."

The Salt Lake Herald, June 09, 1898
Salt Lake City Utah

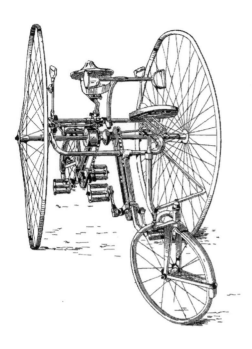

"I have invented certain new and useful improvements in

Tandem Velocipedes.

By arranging the frames to which the seats are attached on opposite sides of the center of the axle the seats are thrown out of line, and the rear rider has an unobstructed view of the road in front of the machine, which not only affords the pleasure of seeing the objects along the line of travel, but enables the rider to apprehend any approaching danger incident to bad places in the road – such as obstructions, gullies, or approaching vehicles. Furthermore, by placing both seats out of the median line of the machine it (the machine) is evenly balanced and runs true and smooth."

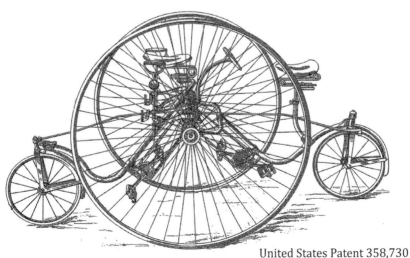

United States Patent 358,730
Inventor: CILLEY, JOHN H.
Date: March 1, 1887

THE VELOCIPEDE

The coming thing is the velocipede. Certainly it is one of the funniest, queerest and most interesting machines that has been invented, and upon the whole it is worthy to succeed base-ball in the affections of the young men of the country. There are almost as many styles of velocipedes as of four-wheeled carriages, and they will multiply rapidly. We understand that there are nearly fifty patterns on exhibition at the Patent Office. The only velocipede worth talking about are the two-wheeled ones. There are three and four-wheeled machines, but of course there is more friction to overcome in running three or four wheels than in running two wheels, and there is no trouble in arrranging for the application of the whole strength of a strong man to the two-wheeled machine.

The Weekly Caucasian
Lexington, Lafayette County, Mo.
February 27, 1869

"**My** invention is an **improvement in velocipedes**, and has for an object, among others, to provide a velocipede which may be driven by the hands of the operator and in which the grips held in the hands may be moved to set the clutch devices into and out of adjustment to key the wheels upon the drive-shaft.   The invention has for a further object to provide an **adjustable platform** to form a support for the operator, which platform may be conveniently raised and lowered by the operator while the velocipede is in use. "

Inventor: Neubert, E.H.

December 4, 1890

7

The number of cripples riding bicycles in New York city is quite noticeable. The progress made in building wheels has done much to improve the construction of cripple carriages, and the borrowing of ideas seems to be reacting, so that instead of putting bicycle features into carts, true bicycles are being adapted for the use of persons maimed in different ways. The one-legged man, the lame man and others can get over the ground on a bike just as fast as any one, providing that one leg can be used. For cripples who have lost the power of their lower limbs hand-propelled bicycles are provided in the place of the more cumbersome tricycles.

The Saint Paul Globe, May 22, 1898
St. Paul, Minn.

"THIS invention has for its object the devising of a practical and simple form of bicycle which may be **propelled by the hands** through power applied to a lever which also serves as a means by which the vehicle may be steered; and our principal endeavor in the invention has been to make this propelling-level serve the double purpose stated.   We thus provide a form of bicycle or similar pleasure-vehicle wherein the **arms of the rider are exercised**, and which is adapted to those who cannot, for physical reasons, operate pedals with their feet."

Publication number   US439922 A
Publication type   Grant
Publication date   November 4, 1890
Inventors   Elleet W. Wood

MEDICAL VIEW OF BICYCLING

The advantages of wheel riding may be inestimable, if practiced intelligently and with moderation, but harmful or absolutely dangerous if carried to excess or in cases where riding should be prohibited. The advantages accruing to riders are obvious, since the wheel affords exercise and recreation to the mentally over-worked, and as an independent and inexpensive means of location it is ideal. The danger of the wheel may consist of injuries from accident, inflammation of the knee joint resulting from overwork, inflammation of both male and female pelvic organs resulting from pressure of the saddle, etc. Another danger is in the con-stant excessive exertion, which can produce an increased atomic and molecular change throughout the body, especially in the vital organs, to such a degree that a general weakening of the individual and an especial susceptibility to infectious diseases may result. The tendency to catch cold is provided by experience to be great. The heart is subject to the greatest danger in cases of the excessive cycle riding. A large number of sudden deaths have already been recorded, due to excessive strain on the heart.

Cases where wheeling should be prohibited are as follows: (1) Ex-isting heart lesions, (2) Arterial calsification, (3) Albuminuria, (4) Old age, and (5) Childhood.

Sacramento Record-Union, October 12, 1897

"**This** invention relates to bicycles in general, and more particu-larly to that class which are **adapted to be driven by both the hands and the feet of the rider;**

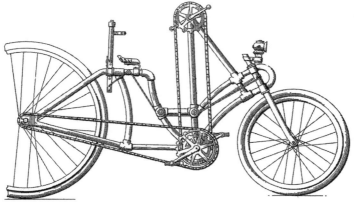

and the objects of the invention are to provide a construction for efficiently conveying the motion to the drive-wheel of the bicycle and also to provide simple and efficient means for steering the bicycle, it being of course understood that the principles involved may be embodied in a similar vehicle of any specific style."

United States Patent 0664274
Inventor; KERR GEORGE G (US)
Application Number: US1900017126A
Filing Date: May 18, 1900

2. AFLOAT & ALOFT

MISS FLORENCE BARRETT. She won the mile water-bicycle race held in New York City. It started at the Battery and finished at Midland Beach

Central News Photo

Evening Public Ledger,
Philadelphia, Pa.
July 14, 1921

13

A MARINE VELOCIPEDE

Last winter a young Chicago genius took out a patent for an ice bicycle and now there is another at work on a marine bicycle. A machine of this nature has been patented within the last few weeks by a New Orleans man. He calls it a marine velocipede.

The News and Herald, Winnsboro, S.C., June 22, 1895

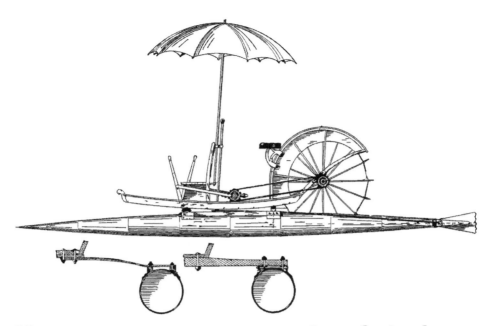

"**My** invention relates to improvements in **marine velocipedes**, and its object is to provide the same with certain new and useful features.

The [drawing]represents two substantially **cigar shaped floats**, arranged a suitable distance apart and parallel with each other, and preferably made of galvanized iron riveted and soldered, which floats constitute the boat proper. These floats support a body having any convenient-shape; that shown being of a small flat bottomed skiff.

A rudder of suitable form is pivoted to the rear end of each float, and said rudders are operated by suitable wires which are attached to eyes at each side of the rudders and extend forward along the surface of the floats to the transverse arms of the crosses.

A staff to support an umbrella, flagw, or sail, passes through an opening in the bracket and rests at its lower end in a socket secured to the sea.

The device shown is adapted to be operated by two persons. One upon the seat operates the levers by the hands, and the other, upon the seat operates the crank shaft with the feet on the pedals and with the hands steers the device by means of the handles and parts connecting the same with the rudders."

Publication number: US540680 A
Publication date: June 11, 1895
Inventor :   V. Moulton

15

BICYCLE TO TRAVEL ON WATER

A unique device produced by a Jersey City inventor is a water bicycle. At first sight the machine looks like a bicycle with sleigh runners instead of wheels; but it carries, also, two large air tanks to support both machine and rider. It is said to be nonsinkable.

The Kentuckian (Hopkinsville, KY), May 24, 1919

WATER BICYCLE MAKES HIT AT CONEY ISLAND

The machines are sustained in the water by tanks, the head and shoulders of the rider being above water, pedals like those on an ordinary bicycle work the propeller and the machine is capacable of making good speed.

South Bend News Times, May 15, 1921

16

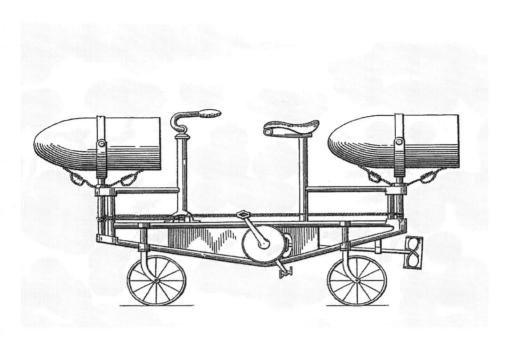

"**This** invention relates to improvements in **bicycle boats.**

In carrying out the present invention, it is my purpose to provide a device of the class described wherein by means of floats, the apparatus maybe

buoyed up by the water and wherein the floats may be operated to steer the apparatus, thereby eliminating the necessity of employing a rudder or similar steering device.

It is also my purpose to provide apparatus of the type set forth which may

be **propelled through the water** after the fashion of a bicycle and which may be steered easily and conveniently and wherein the component parts will be so arranged and correlated as to reduce the possibility of derangement to a minimum."

Patent: US1206587A
Inventor: Lewis Peterson
Publication date: November 28, 1916

Like Nothing Ever Before Invented - It is Proving The
Greatest Fad The French Capial Has Seen in Years -
Physicians Enthuse Over It -
The Peculiar Motion Makes It Remarkable In The Aid It
Gives To Health

THE NEW FRENCH AQUATIC SEXTET

Girls Spin Along River Seine In A Sextuplet Affair

A sextuplet affair, the six girls who ride it have the jolliest of times. ... The ordinary bicycle boat has done very well when with all the impetus the riders could give it made four miles an hour. The latest invention has done fifteen miles an hour, and there is no indication whatever that the limit has been reached.

The Kentuckian, April 16, 1919
Hopkinsville, Ky.

"**Be** it known that I, GUSTAV SWAN, a citizen of Norway, residing at Sioux Falls, in the county of Minnehaha and State of South Dakota, have invented certain new and useful **Improvements in Bicycle Boats**, of which the following is a specification.

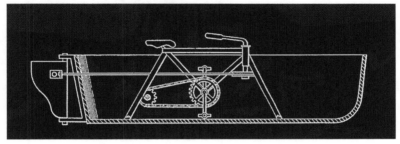

This invention relates to improvements in bicycle boats. One object is to provide a boat of this type in which the driving and steering parts are so arranged that it is possible to readily drive the boat forward or backward or to cause it to turn as upon a pivot in order to effect a perfect landing without particular effort on the part of the operator.

A further object is to provide a novel boat of this type that is cheap to manufacture and simple and efficient in operation."

United States Patent 1459297
Inventor: Gustave, Swan
Publication Date: June 19,1923

FLOATING BICYCLE

The latest water novelty is the water bicycle. It is operated by pedals, with a propeller; is non-sinkable and can attain a speed of 5 miles.

Richmond Times Dispatch, June 26, 1921

WATER BICYCLE NEWEST OF GERMAN INVENTIONS

Mr. Otto William, who has completed a cross country tour of Germany on his waterwheel. From the north of Germany, Herr William proceeded alongtheprincipal waterways to South Germany, attracting crowds along the route. The contrivance is similar to an ordinary bicycle, except that paddles, attached tothegear, propel the machine. The prime essential is a good supply of leg power.

The Chickasha Daily Express, February 11, 1922

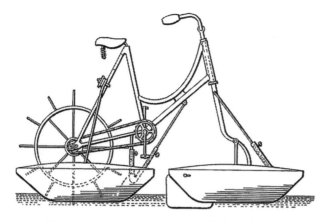

"**An** object of the invention is to provide means whereby the usual frame of a bicycle may be mounted upon a series of pontoons and a rider may mount the frame and use the pedals of the bicycle for rotating a propelling wheel which is journaled at the rear portion of the frame and whereby the device is propelled over the surface of a body of water.

The style or pattern of the bicycle frame is immaterial and the pontoons may be filled with air or not as desired as they possess sufficient buoyancy to keep the device afloat. If air is used additional buoyancy is imparted to the pontoons and in the event of leakage the escaping air will disclose the points of leakage at the surfaces of the pontoon.

A further object of the invention is to provide a forward pontoon adapted to be attached to the steering shaft of the bicycle frame and which pontoon is provided with a rudder adapted to guide the device when the steering shaft is turned and the device is being propelled."

United States Patent 1920391
Inventor: Herwig, Ernest C. L.
Application Number: US63201932A
Publication Date: August 1, 1933

Walks and Rides on Water

Prof. Alphonso King, the great marine performer, gives an exhibition at Lake Harriet this afternoon at 4 p.m. and at 7:30 p.m. in the evening. This is the man who actually walks on the water and also rides a bicycle on the paddles, and surmounted by a saddle like that of the ordinary bicycle. The machine is a very ingenious contrivance.

St. Paul Daily Globe, June 8, 1889, Saint Paul, Minn.

"**The** purpose of this invention is to provide an improvement in unicycles whereby they are adapted for use in the water for sports, amusement, fishing, **water polo**, and the like, and which, when used, will stand upright and support a person in the upright position.

The invention is a unicycle embodying a relatively large tubular wheel with a weighted keel extending downward therefrom, and with a seat and rotating means extending upward, in which the wheel has sufficient buoyancy to support a person on the seat, and the keel is sufficient to hold the seat in an upright position.

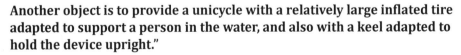

The object of this invention is, therefore, to improve cycles of the type adapted to be used in the water, and, particularly, of the type having one wheel, such as a unicycle by providing means for positively holding the device upright with a person on the upper end.

Another object is to provide a unicycle with a relatively large inflated tire adapted to support a person in the water, and also with a keel adapted to hold the device upright."

Inventor: Nilsson, Walter E.
Application Number: US25375439A
Publication Date: August 15, 1939

23

"This invention relates to improvements in **bicycle boats** and has for its object to provide a simple and efficient means of travel on water.

I claim:

a bicycle boat comprising two floats;

a frame connecting said two floats;

a sprocket-wheel mounted in said frame;

pedals secured to said sprocket-wheel;

a shaft connecting said two floats near the front end thereof;

a sprocket-wheel revolubly mounted on said shaft and having square sockets in opposite ends thereof;

two paddle wheels revolubly mounted on said shaft each having a square boss on one end to fit into the square socket of the sprocket-wheel hub;

collars rigidly secured to said shaft adjacent the paddle;

heels to hold them securely to the sprocket-wheel; and

means mounted in said frame for guiding the boat."

Inventor: Perry, Elwood R.
Application Number: US40929541A
Publication Date: June 23, 1942

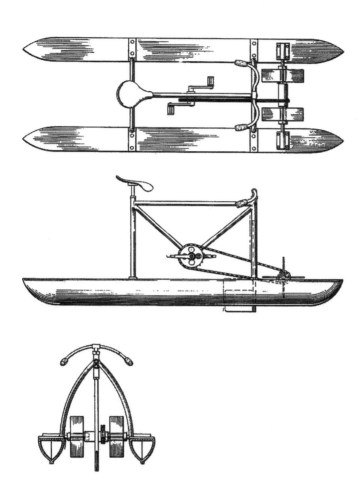

AERIAL BICYCLE

There is a likelihood that the problem of rapid transit has been solved by Hiram Mikarsonof Stroughton, Mass. He has invented an apparatus that he calls the "aerial bicycle" although it travels on a rail.

The rail for this apparatus is on a post that curves outward several feet at the top, and the rider sails along beneath the rail. Two wheels run on the rail. They are connected by a tailpiece,to which is fastened a framwork that extends downward.

At the end of this framwork is a propelling mechanism, seat and handle being very much like an ordinary bicycle. The pedals are driven in the ordinary way, and power is commuicated to the wheels above by an endless chain that passes along the framework and over one of the hubs.

Such a railway would be very cheap to build, and it has the advantage of not taking up any ground to speak of, as crops can be grown between the posts. Considerable speed ought to be developed with very little power.

Phillipsburg Herald., June 07, 1901
Phillipsburg, Kan.

AN IDEA FOR LAZY WHEELMEN

Unique Project for a Bicycle Trolley to Be Erected for Easy Transit Along Main Highways.

CYCLING MADE EASY.

The Progress., August 14, 1897, Page 15
Shreveport, La.

An object of my invention is to provide a trolley-bicycle adapted to be run upon an ordinary dirt road by an electric motor, but without rails and without being handicapped by the weight of a battery or an individual generator of electricity.

To this end it consists of a specially-organized bicycle carrying an electric motor and having the front portion of its framework extended upwardly in the form of a trolley-pole bearing two trolley wheels adapted to run against two conducting wires oppositely charged and having two corresponding wires running from the two trolley-wheels down the trolley-pole to the opposite poles of the motor.

The said bicycle being provided with the usual pedals for operation by the feet of the rider, when desired, and the trolley-pole being joined to fold up, so that the bicycle may be operated in the usual way over any road and independently of the electric conduction-wires, when desired, or be geared to the conducting-wires to run the bicycle by electric power, or the power and pedal mechanism may both be made available at the same time, as might in some cases be desirable, as in climbing hills or in emergencies where the power of the electric current or the effectiveness of the motor might be accidentially diminished."

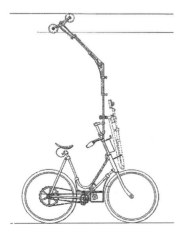

Publication number US588465 A
Publication date   Aug 17, 1897
Inventors   Robert T. Oney

29

A BICYCLE TROLLEY

A brand new idea has just been sprung upon the wheeling world. The inventor claims that it is destined to double-discount the motor bicycle and the horseless carriage.

His plan is to apply to bicycles the same motive power which has been so successfully used for streetcars - not with the idea of discarding the present method of propelling the wheel by means of pedals, but to enable the wheelman to coast through the main thoroughfares without effort by means of the trolley, reserving his strength for crossroads and bypaths, where the trolley line is not laid.

If the wheelman is riding to reduce his weight or develop his muscles, and therefore prefers to supply the motive power himself, he can do so as readily with the trolley bicycle as with an ordinary wheel; but should he tire and wish to spin home as comfortably and indolently as though riding in a streetcar, he has only to hitch his machine to the trolley line, and away he will go, fast or slow, as he pleases, wtihout the slightest exertion.

The idea of the patentee is to have special trolley wires for bicycles erected on the most important country roads adjoining cities and in some of the main streets of the cities.

New York Tribune, October 31, 1897

"**My** invention relates to a new and useful improvement in monocycles or suspended vehicles, and has for its object to provide a simple and effective apparatus which may be utilized-after the manner of a bicycle, but traveling upon an overhead wire, for the transportation of one or more persons, and which may be either propelled by crank mechanism operated by the occupants or by a suitable motor.

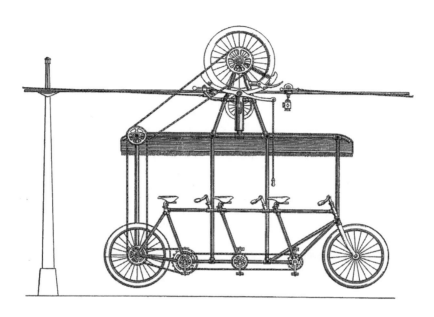

I have provided three seats in order to accommodate three riders and with the further object of permitting the balancing of the machine when but two riders are mounted or even but a single rider is using the device.

The apparatus maybe readily suspended from the line-wire, which should be arranged above the surface of the country over which it is stretched sufficiently to insure the clearance of the wheels and by one or more riders mounting the proper seats it may be propelled forward at a considerable rate of speed, and when the destination of the rider is reached it may be detached from the line wire and then used as a surface vehicle after the manner of a tricycle by uncoupling the clutch , which will cut off the motion from the traction-wheel and permit the entire power of the rider to be utilized in giving the machine progression upon the surface."

Publication number   US599697 A
Publication type   Grant
Publication date   March 1, 1898
Inventors   George S. Foster

31

THE BICYCLE TROLLEY

Detriot Inventor Has An Idea Which
Is Interesting Even Thought It May
Not Be Practical

WHEELING
ON A WIRE.

Bicycle Trolley. Invented by a
Detroit Genius, the Latest
Thing In Transportation.

If the dreams of a Detroit inventor are
realized there will soon be a network
of wires streching across the country
on which owners of bicycles will be
able to travel at their ease and without
paying any attention to the condition
of the roads. The invention, as the
Detroit man has patented it, consists
of a steel frame suspended from a
wire, the frame being so built that it
will hold an ordinary bicycle, together with the necessary mechanism
for communicating the power to the
wheels running on the trolley wire.

Richmond Planet., July 07, 1900
Richmond, Va.

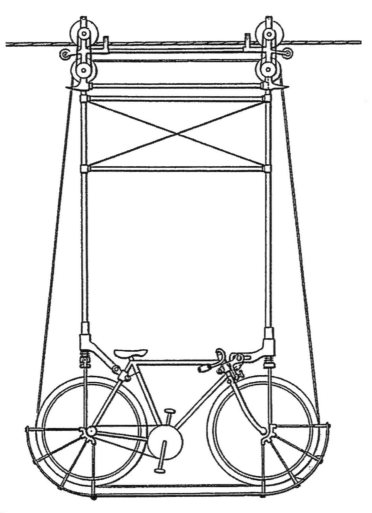

"**My** invention relates to means for mounting a bicycle in a suitable frame or car suspended from an overhead trolley wire or rail, whereby the bicycle when operated by a rider becomes the motor for propelling the car along the wire."

Inventor: Talbot, James H.
Application Number: US638,296
Publication Date: December 5, 1899

3. ONE, TWO AND MORE WHEELS

LAITNER & MONROE.

The San Francisco Call., November 21, 1896

In conclusion, it may be stated that though the velocipede disease is now raging so fearfully as to make it appear that the epidemic is doomed to run eternally, yet when we remember that the affair has often before been brought forward under the most favorable of circumstances and as often has sunk out of sight again, we can only believe that within another twelve months it will once more disappear from the public gaze. In the meantime give it every possible chance. Trundle it around skating rinks, roll it about the stages of leading theaters, let it 'scoot"'along the smoothest sections of pavement to be found, and still its glories shall assuredly wane in the end, and having finally faded from popular notice, the captivating plaything will eventually be obliged to seek retirement for another twenty years.

Chicago Times, October 18, 1868

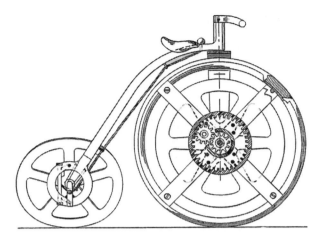

"**My** invention consists of a gyroscopic wheel fitted into the driving or guide wheel of a velocipede, and sleeved on the shaft of said driving-wheel, and adapted to rotate with greater rapidity than said driving-wheel.

The gyroscopic power derived serving to increase the ease of operation of the velocipede, impart uniformity of motion thereof, and prevent overturning of the same.

The rider occupies the seat and operates the cranks so as to impact motion to the wheel. As the wheel is carried around with the hub or disk, and as it gears with the toothed rim, it rotates on its axis and imparts rotation to the center pinion, which, owing to the tooth or pawl, rotates the gyroscopic wheel, the speed of which is greater than the wheel.

By this provision the velocipede may be run with great rapidity and ease, the motion is uniform, and the liability of overturning is overcome, due to the gyroscopic impulse of the wheel."

Publication number US236259 A
Publication date   Jan 4, 1881
Inventors   Joseph Reid

37

NOVEL WAR MACHINE.

A Device for Transporting Troops at Rapid Rates.

Medical science continues to invent new methods of saving life, and military science new engines of destruction, and similarly each modern improvement in transporting

INFANTRY ON MULTICYCLE.

things for the good of mankind is contemporary with improved transportation for killing purposes. Among the many new devices for the latter purpose the most novel is the so called multicycle—a sort of compound velocipede by which a squad of soldiers may all move together, have their baggage or ammunition with them and have a ready made breastwork when they stop. We present engravings of the machine in action and serving as a slight defense to the legs of the soldiers. The machine has been tried on the streets of London with apparent success, and is now being severely tested at Aldershot by authority of the British War office. It is called a multicycle because it usually carries twelve men and can be constructed to take sixteen.

Bismarck Weekly Tribune., June 03, 1887
Bismarck, N.D.

"My invention relates to certain new and useful improvements in bicycles, and has for one object, primarily, the production of what I denominate a multicycle, which may be added to for the purpose of increasing its carrying capacity, and when arranged as hereinafter set forth may; be divided or separated to constitute a number of individual tandems.

It has for a further object to provide a machine in which every wheel constituting the multicycle, with the exception of the first of the series, shall become a steering-wheel, whereby a movement analogous to that of a snake may, when desired, be imparted to the machine.

It has for a further object to so construct and connect the several/unitary sections that each of the riders will receive but one momentum shock when the machine encounters ordinary obstructions, and that the machine throughout its length may have a vertically undulatory motion in order that it may accommodate itself to the uneven surface of the roadway.

It has for a further object to lessen the slipping friction of the driving-wheels existing in all bicycles carrying more than two riders by dispensing with all devices of any character whatever for transmitting the motive force from two or more fixed localities to one common driving-wheel."

Publication number   US647785 A
Publication date   Apr 17, 1900
Inventors   James C Anderson

TWO SAILORS OFF ON
TANDEM SPRINT

Early last evening many people on the streets saw two smiling blue jackets aboard a tandem bicycle.   They did not appear to be steering any direct course, but seemed to tack back and forth in irregular lines across the streets, bowing to everyone in sight and making life as merry as possible for themselves.

About 5 o'clock M.G. Sousa entered the police station and complained that a green tandem bicycle that had been left standing in front of Morris' bicycle shop on Fort street had been stolen.

The police put two and two together and then decided that the sailors better be run in if they still had the machine on the streets.   Officers were instructed to keep an eye peeled for them.

The Pacific Commercial Advertiser,
Honolulu, HI, November 13, 1902

"**My** invention relates to certain new and useful improvements in bicycles, and especially to that class known as **tandems**, and which are designed to carry two riders, both of whom cooperate to propel the machine.

My invention has for its prime object to provide a wheel of such construction that each and both wheels shall be essentially driving wheels and that the riders shall each be mounted directly over the axis of his respective wheel, and thus be able to apply his power in the most effective manner.

My invention has for another object to provide a novel steering device in tandem construction whereby the front rider controls the path of travel of the wheel over which the rear rider is mounted, ... and hence the forward and steering rider upon any of my improved wheels, applying the same handle-bar movement with which he may have been accustomed, secures the proper trend of the tandem without any confusion to himself."

Publication number   US647786 A
Publication date   Apr 17, 1900
Inventors   James C Anderson

"**Among** the principal objects which the present invention has in view are:

To provide an improved unicycle; To provide means whereby the operator can operate the unicycle without the necessity of applying his hand or foot externally of the apparatus; To utilize a relative actuation between two wheels in propelling the apparatus; To employ a brake for bringing the apparatus to a stop; To provide means whereby the apparatus can jump and/or hurdle over objects in the road; To enable the apparatus to be passed over obstacles without requiring the operator to first bring the apparatus to a stop or remove himself from the apparatus; To attach the various parts making up the mechanism to the inside wheel of the apparatus; To provide means between the two wheels whereby the wheels may have a relative rotation one with respect to the other; and To secure simplicity of construction and operation.

When momentum has been obtained the operator then leaps onto the seat, places his right foot on the foot rest treadle, then moves his body in a forward motion and at the same time applies pressure on the foot rest treadle, that is to say the toe portion of the foot presses down on the forward part of said foot rest thereby causing the U-shaped member to engage with the revolving wheel. The operator also swings his body forward during this clutch-engaging period, causing both wheels to rotate together through a short distance, after which he releases so the clutch pressure and rocks his body rearwardly, during which time the wheels are rotating in opposite directions, the outer one continuing the forward rotation at all times. The forward and backward movement of the operator's body permits propelling and added speed to the apparatus.

Should the operator desire to retard forward movement of the apparatus or stop it, he straightens his body which then engages with a member. In pressing against this member, the said member is adapted frictionally to hold the inner wheel in contact with the outer wheel thereby preventing relative rotation between the two wheels.

An added feature of the present invention is that when the apparatus is in motion it may be caused to hurdle over holes or objects in the road, thereby giving added thrills to the user."

United States Patent 2019728
Inventor: Ranck, John V.
Application Number: US71908034A
Publication Date: 11/05/1935

"**This** invention relates to vehicles of the type having a single supporting and driving wheel, known as unicycles, and more particularly to power means and control means for vehicles of this type, arranged to be operated by a rider for driving and braking said vehicle as well as maintaining balance thereof.

Prior art unicycles are powered by the rider through conventional foot pedals which are connected to the single supporting wheel. The circular motion of the feet required to **transmit torque** to the single supporting wheel, adds considerably to the problem of maintaining balance. Consequently, long hours of intense practice are required to obtain the necessary balance in riding a unicycle. Also, riding a conventional unicycle is very tiring and the speed and accelerations which can be obtained are low, thereby limiting the thrill of riding.

Accordingly, as an overall object, the present invention seeks to provide an engine driven one-wheeled vehicle that can be easily controlled by the rider to maintain balance.

Another object of the invention is to provide an engine driven one-wheeled vehicle provided with means for enabling the rider to quickly learn to operate the vehicle without falling off and without the vehicle falling to the ground.

Another object of the invention is to provide an engine driven one-wheeled vehicle which may be readily balanced by the rider without the use of a gyroscope of the type which resists changes in the attitude of the vehicle.

A further object of the invention is to provide an engine driven one-wheeled vehicle with rapid acceleration and braking and high maneuverability to provide a sporting ride.

Still another object of the invention is to provide an engine driven one-wheeled vehicle in which the driving and braking torque are controlled by the rider from a single manually operated linear motion or pressure actuated proportional controller."

Publication number   US3399742 A
Publication type Grant
Publication date Sep 3, 1968
InventorFranklin S Malick

THE TANDEM BICYCLE.

The Latest Invention for Those Who Enjoy the Wheel—A Tandem Bicycle for Ladies.

The latest thing for lovers is the lady's tandem bicycle. It is an English idea, none the less popular in this country on that account. In Brooklyn, Boston, Washington and other cities where there are good pavements it is rapidly coming into vogue. Its construction is, in the main, similar to that of the ordinary safety machine, the wheels being similar and propelled by gearing connected with the pedals.

The front wheel is considerably smaller than the main wheel, and the seats are on standards low and strong. The lady's seat is between the two wheels a little back of the center of the machine. The gentleman's seat is over the large wheel in the rear. Upon him devolves the greater part of the duty of propulsion and the guidance of the vehicle. The lady has hand rests by which to make her seat more firm, but has

nothing to do with steering the machine. Her pedals gear with those of her companion, and a high rate of speed is easily possible.

All the advantages of safety machines are secured, and the tandem is a very delightful machine to ride. As a matter of fact, bicycles are far safer than tricycles, and some of the most terrible accidents that have occurred to ladies in the pastime of wheeling have occurred to those riding tricycles. They are bulky, hard to steer, slow of speed, confusing in their movements and liable to frightful headers on bad pavements. The safety tandem has never been known to break any limbs.

Wichita Eagle, January 23, 1889
Wichita, Kan.

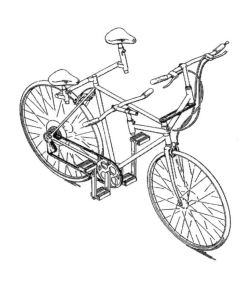

"**In** order for a bicycle to carry more than one person at a time, it has been customary in some instances to arrange the riders in tandem and in other instances to arrange the riders side by side.

This latter arrangement is in many respects preferred but has some difficulty in that the riders tend to have their centers of mass a substantial distance away from the median, vertical, longitudinal plane of the bicycle and also tend to interfere with each other in the operation of the vehicle.

To keep the centers of gravity close to the center of the machine and to arrange for little or no interference between the riders, it is presently arranged so that the riders' seats can be longitudinally staggered and maintained at different heights; and it is also arranged so that the handle bars can be set at different locations in a fore and aft direction and likewise at different heights.

The riders, although seated generally side by side, can be in effect vertically and longitudinally somewhat spaced apart so as partially at least to interfit transversely. This is particularly advantageous if the riders are disparate in size, skill or physical ability; e.g. should one of the riders be handicapped.

The steering is preferably arranged to be done by one rider only with the other rider being given handle bars of a nonrotatable nature. The pedaling is provided for by two pairs of cranked pedals arranged respectively on opposite sides of the central, longitudinal plane of the vehicle. With this construction the riding is compact, well balanced, without interference and easy."

Inventors: Barrett, Robert C.
Application Number: 05/835305
Publication Date: 12/11/1979

4. COSTUMES

One-third of the bicycles sold in 1895 were for women's use. In 1894 the women's bicycle were only five per cent of the males.

Wheels Not For Women

Mrs. Kendal Says Bicycling Ruins
a Girl's Health and Features

Mrs. Kendal has written an article on women bicycle riders in which she says: 'Riding astride a horse, a camel - any animal - is not feminine, and never will be so, according to the laws of nature. Bicycle riding is a violence exercise. Can it be good for women? If a girl of 16 is to do exactly what the boy of that age does, bicycling is more harmful to her than a dozen other rough sports the male has always enjoyed. But can a girl of 16 do what her brother does without endangering her health? I say she cannot.

"When a girl gets astride her bicycle she bids farewell to her good looks. If she develops new muscles be sure some other parts of her suffer, some faculty will be alighted, some natural trait undeveloped.

As for bloomers, they are abominable."

Hutchinson Gazette., July 11, 1895
Hutchinson, Kansas

The officials that undertake to arrest women bicycle riders who wear bloomers will have anything but a happy time of it, and will have to retreat with the jeers of the entire country at their folly. They don't seem to know American women.

The Broad Ax., November 12, 1896
Salt Lake City, Utah

The bicycle is doing more to bring about dress reform than centuries of exhortation, even accompanied by heroic example by Mrs. Bloomer, could accomplish.

The Scranton Tribune, October 13,
1895

50

"**This** invention relates to improvements in skirts or suits worn by ladies, and while it may be employed in their dress for various occasions and purposes, yet it is more especially adapted for use in athletic costumes, such as are worn when riding bicycles."

"The object of my invention is to provide a skirt to be worn over knickerbockers, trousers, or bloomers, and which may be readily drawn up into graceful flounces or gathers near the waste of the wearer and at the rear thereof and also partly drawn up in front to about the knees or a little above them, so that the skirt will offer no hindrance or obstruction to the motion of the legs when operating the pedals of the wheel or bicycle."

Johnson, Frank A.
Letters Patent No. 548,613
October 22, 1895

"I think it [bicycling] has done more to emancipate women than anything else in the world. It gives women a feeling of freedom and self-reliance. I stand and rejoice every time I see a woman ride by on a wheel...the picture of free, untrammeled womanhood."

Susan B. Anthony

Great Falls Daily Tribune
July 04, 1920

"The question now of great interest to girls is in regard to the healthfulness of the wheel. Many are prophesying dire results from this fascinating exercise, and fond parents are refusing to allow their daughters to ride because they are girls. It will be a delight to girls to learn that the fact of their sex is, in itself, not a bar to riding a wheel. If the girl is normally constituted and is dressed hygienically, and if she will use judgment and not overtax herself in learning to ride, and in measuring the length of rides after she has learned, she is in no more danger from riding a wheel than is the young man. But if she persists in riding in a tight dress, and uses no judgment in deciding the amount of exercise she is capable of safely taking, it will be quite possible for her to injure herself, and then it is she, and not the wheel, that is to blame. Many physicians are now coming to regard the 'wheel' as beneficial to the health of women as well as of men."   Dr. Seneca Egbert

A WHEEL Within A WHEEL, by Frances E. Willard, 1895.

"**My** invention has reference to skirts for women bicycle-riders, and has for its object to produce a skirt which can in a moment be converted from a walking-skirt into a bicycle skirt, the latter possessing all the advantages of **Turkish trousers or bloomers** and the former having the appearance of an ordinary walking-skirt.

As a new article of manufacture, the combination walking and bicycle skirt herein described, consisting of a full skirt-body, fastening devices upon the front breadth at the bottom, complemental fastening devices on the back breadth opposite thereto, means secured to the skirt opposite each ankle of the wearer for fastening the same to the legs of the wearer and means secured to the skirt at the upper and lower portions thereof for drawing the lower portion of the skirt upward, whereby the single structure may, at the will of the wearer, be allowed to fall around both legs as a skirt, or be drawn up to the crotch to form a pair of trousers, as set forth."

J. H. DEUTSCHMAN
Letters Patent No. 557,495
Dated March 31, 1896

The wheel costume of the woman rider has always been a source of much trial and travail. It is really a difficult problem to adjust all the conflicting features of skirt-length, skirt fullness, comfort, appearance and practicability into such a combination as shall be satisfactory on all points.

The Los Angeles Herald
August 11, 1895

New-York Tribune., March 25, 1898

BICYCLE COSTUME.

"This invention relates to skirts of riding habits for women, and, while adapted equally for use upon the conventional sidesaddle for horseback-riding, is adapted for use upon bicycles, as well as for walking and house skirts.

It is acknowledged that the most picturesque and generally desirable skirt for use upon a bicycle is what is known as an ordinary round skirt, but various objections attend the use of the same, and therefore bloomers and what are known as divided skirts have come somewhat into use.

One of the principal objections to the ordinary round skirt lies in the fact that the rider must gather and raise the same at the back in order to properly sit upon the bicycle, and this leaves an unusual fullness toward the front and either on one side or the other, which is easily caught by the wind, and, thus even in a light wind, the edge of the skirt is being constantly raised, so as to expose to view unnecessarily the limbs of the rider, while in a very strong or head wind the latter gets under the skirt, fills it, and extends it balloon fashion, thus making a very unsightly appearance and also causing great inconvenience to the rider.

Another object of the invention is to provide a skirt which may be sufficiently short in length to enable its convenient use upon a bicycle or upon horseback, and at the same time so fashioned that it may be used as an ordinary walking-skirt without the passer-by suspecting that it has a special configuration model or fashion or that it has been specially made as a riding-habit.

Another object of the invention is to provide a garment whereby the limbs of the wearer thereof shall be absolutely concealed from view from the rear when the wearer is riding a bicycle."

Greenleaf, Agnes Staines
Letters Patent No. 568,943
Dated October 6, 1896

Men's Bicycle Clothing

Just Received
Entirely New Line of

**Bicycle Suits,
Bicycle Hose,
Sweaters,
Caps, Belts, Etc.**

The Nobbiest Line
in Town.

The Seattle Post-Intelligencer, April 18, 1897
Seattle, Wash.

Men's Bicycle Clothing.

Of all Descriptions.

Suits from $2.50 up.

Pants,

$1.50, $2.00, $2.50.

Stockings, 25 Cents.

Mower County Transcript, June 03, 1896
Lansing, Minn.

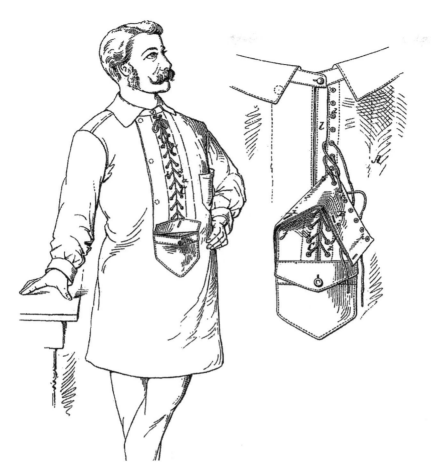

"**This** invention relates to certain improvements in shirts, more particularly the kind known as bicycle-shirts, which is a kind having lacing in front, and has for its object, so far as the bosom part of the shirt is concerned, to allow the shirt to be readily opened and closed without interfering with the lacing, and to provide for one half of the laced portion a face strip or piece which, except at the lower end, is disconnected from the shirt.

The invention also consists in applying a pocket to the shirt directly below the bosom, and in utilizing the usual suspension-strap as a cover for that pocket."

Schneer, Issac
Letters Patent No. 274,520.
Dated March 27, 1883.

57

MISJUDGED

The bronzed and weatherbeaten face of the president of the wheel club was darkened by a shade of disappointment as he laid his hand on the shoulder of the younger member.

"Mr. Pneumo," he said, kindly, "you have been so regular in attendance at our meets and so enthusiastic in all matters pertaining to the welfare of the club, that I dislike to speak to you on a subject that has pained me greatly. But I feel that I must ask of you why it is that you so often appear among us not wearing the regulation bicycle trousers we have adopted and which, it should not be necessary to tell you, are required to be worn on all important occasions." For a moment a deep blush spread over the face of the unfortunate young man thus addressed, and then drawing the elder man to his side, he hastily muttered a few words in his ear. Then it was that the elder man turned and grasped him by the hand, and said in tones of the deepest sympathy: "Will you forgive me? I did not know that you had a sister."

The Eagle, Silver City, N.M.
September 12, 1894

"**My** invention relates to **trousers**; and its object is to provide ordinary trousers with attachments whereby they may be readily converted into knee-pants or knickerbockers.

It is well known that many bicycle-riders are in the habit of riding to their business places in the well-known knickerbocker bicycle-suits, and are compelled to appear in such suits throughout the day.

By the use of my improvements the ease and freedom of knickerbockers is insured while riding, after which the trousers may be readily converted into a pair of trousers of ordinary appearance, the elevating devices being entirely concealed and causing no inconvenience to the wearer."

Hercht, Pauline Grayson
Letters Patent No. 587,310
Dated August 3, 1897

5. ETCETERA

Ride a Bicycle for Health and Pleasure

Ride a Bicycle

Ride a Bicycle. Save Time in Business

NATIONAL BICYCLE WEEK   MAY 4 TO 11

Will be celebrated throughout the United States, to better acquaint the people that the bicycle is still in the race, and not a back number. If the great world's war continues, GASOLINE will be commandeered by the Government and those who drive automobiles will be compelled to use other means of transportation.

We can be patriotic now by riding a Bicycle and saving gasoline

Ride a Bicycle and limber up and increase your earning capacity

Ride a Bicycle and your health will be better---the best of excuse

If the street car service is poor--beat them to it--ride a Bicycle

For economy, convenience and good health--ride a Bicycle

Buy your boy a Bicycle and let him go into the country and help Uncle Sam feed the Army and the poor starving Belgians. The farmers will appreciate the help the boy can give him. The boy can be self-supporting if he RIDES A BICYCLE.

We all can economize in time and energy, and during these times this is a big factor---if we ride a Bicycle. LET'S ALL TOGETHER--RIDE A BICYCLE

Go to your dealer and ask him about the Bicycle--He will tell you a great many things about the Bicycle you never thought of. Next week is Bicycle Week, and the following firms will start you off right:

Scott & Piper
252-260 State Street. Phone 451

A. H. Moore
445 Court Street. Phone 368

Loyd E. Ramsden
221 South High. Phone 1687

Hauser Bros.
272 State Street. Phone 410

126 South Com'l. Phone 363

An invention which will be rather jeered at by seasoned old wheelmen and women is the bicycle umbrella. It is fastened securely to the standard of the handle bar and is intended to keep off both rain and sun. The bicycle enthusiast prides himself on not minding weather of any kind. But some weak hearted riders will like to be protected from getting burned and tanned, even at the cost of a diminution of speed. To these the bicycle umbrella will commend itself. What will it do in a wind, though?

Little Falls Weekly Transcript, November 23, 1894,
Little Falls, Minn.

" **This** invention relates to umbrella supporters, and more especially to that class thereof which are adapted for use on a bicycle or tricycle whereby the entire device becomes

a **cycle canopy**; and the object of the same is to effect improvements in the support 'for canopies of this character.

The present invention contemplates means for supporting this canopy adjustably above the seat of the cycle so that it can be set at any desired angle to prevent sun or rain from striking the rider, and so that it can be raised or lowered or removed entirely when desired."

Publication number   US521619 A
Publication date   Jun 19, 1894
Inventors   William T. Jordan

"**This** invention relates to **driving-backs** for velocipedes and such like, against which the rider presses his back at the same time as he exerts the **muscular force of his legs** upon the pedals, so as to give additional driving power. The driving-back is adjustably secured, under this invention, by means of telescopic tubes, which are hinged to the cycle-frame at the back of the saddle."

No. 636,222.
Patented October 31 1899
E. B. KILLEN.

"**This** invention relates to a **shoulder brace** for bicycle riders, the general object of the invention being to provide an attachment for the bicycle which has means for engaging the shoulders of the rider so as to **eliminate fatigue** as it helps the rider to hold a restful position on the bicycle. Another object of the invention is to provide means for adjusting the device to suit different sizes of riders."

Inventor: Taulbee, Daniel M.
Application Number: US35550440A
Publication Date: 01/28/1941

"**The** application of the device requires little skill or care. It is applied by an upward movement, thrusting the tubes each into the corresponding nostril, and then by the obvious movement of the upper end of the device rearward toward the head the clamping-spring opens a little and allows the clamp to take a gentle hold on the upper portion of the nose. It may be shifted a little from time to time; but my experiments indicate that the wearer soon becomes so accustomed to it that he is unconscious of its pressure. In vigorous exercise, running, rowing, or **working a bicycle** against a strong wind or up a hill this device aids to form and maintain the habit of great importancethat of keeping the lips closed, so that the lungs receive no air except through the nose.

Athletes not requiring spectacles with lenses may wear spectacle-frames with plain glasses or without glasses to obtain this means of doubly assuring the retention of my device."

"**The** invention consists of a pair of **adjustable reflectors** attached or connected to a pair of spectacles or mud-guards in such manner that the relation between the eyes and the reflectors will remain unchanged, whereby objects in the rear will be reflected, thus enabling the wearer to see what is behind while he is looking in a forward direction; and the invention is particularly adapted for races-- such as horse, bicycle, and boat-and also for ordinary roadwork.

By means of spectacles having adjustable reflectors attached to them in the manner described the relation between the eye and the reflectors remain unchanged in whatever the position of the head of the wearer may be, for as his head is moved so are the reflectors. Thus objects in the rear are reflected so as to be seen by the eye when the wearer is looking forward.

This is particularly advantageous in all kinds of races, for often the foremost man loses the race by simply turning his head to see the position of his competitors."

Publication number
US675275 A
Publication type   Grant
Publication date   May 28, 1901

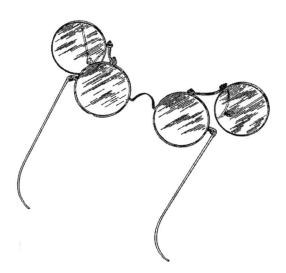

Allan Taylor
Patent No. 614,673
Dated November 22, 1898

6. ENTERTAINING

WALTER SMITH, 16-YEAR-OLD BOY, MAY BE AMERICA'S FASTEST RIDER.

Recently Set Amateur Record for One Mile Paced at 1 Minute 28 Seconds, and Won Ten Mile Amateur Championship Paced Contest—He Is Deemed the Match of All the Big Riders.

WALTER SMITH RIDING A MILE IN 1 M. 28 S.

America has a new phenomena, this time in the shape of a
16-year old boy who can ride a mile behind a motor in 1 minute
and 28 seconds, beating all amateur records. He is Walter
Smith, of the Brookly, N.Y. High School. He weighs 100
pounds and cycling experts given him the equal of any star
in the county. The little fellow's method resembles that of
Jimmy Michael.

The Butte InterMountain
July 25, 1901

ONLY BIG SHOW COMING THIS YEAR

See the bicycle whirl. Most daring and thrilling act ever produced, performed by the famous Slater Family, champion trick bicyclists of the world.

The Socorro Chieftain, Socorro, N.M., June 7, 1902

"**My** present invention relates to an improvement in bicycle-whirls, and has for its object the production of a whirl giving certain capabilities of independent movement to the individual bicycles adapted to be propelled by the riders, which is more agreeable to the riders, more perfect in construction, and capable of nicer adjustment and of great durability than machines of this character heretofore in use.

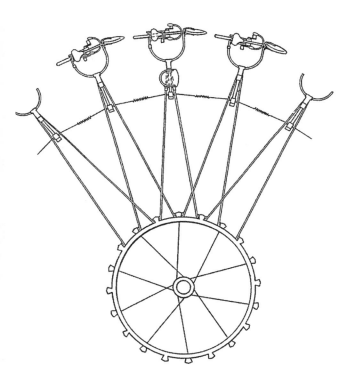

Bicycles of ordinary construction are arranged in a circle around the supporting-frame, each being supported by one of the yokes in any suitable manner. Upon the head of the bicycle-frame is securely fixed the head-clamp. Similarly fixed upon the seat-post of the bicycle-frame is the seat-post clamp, which is provided with a rearwardly-projected ear which passesout between the rear forks of the frame and is then turned to one side.

In order that the bicycles may run properly in the predetermined circular path, I have provided means for setting and holding the front fork in its proper position."

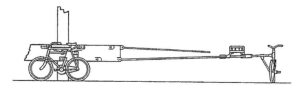

United States Patent 0634857
Inventor: SMITH PERCY L (US)
Grant Date: October 10, 1899

"This invention aims to provide a **novel amusement device** or apparatus to be used by a rider of bicycles and the like.

Prior to my invention what is known as the **"bicycle-whirl"** has been devised and used, consisting of a generally conical and sometimes in part cylindrical inclosure, usually of upright slats, in which the operator rides the bicycle in a circle, gradually climbing the sides of the whirl until he is riding around with his body and machine nearly or quite in a horizontal plane, centrifugal force keeping him in position.

United States Patent 0762232
Inventor: ECK THOMAS W (US)
Application Number: US1904187910A
Filing Date: September 1, 1904

My present invention relates generally to an apparatus used in this manner, and comprehends a spherical hollow whirl or cage within which the rider visibly operates or performs. My invention also comprehends mounting this spherical or, in fact, any whirl so that it may be moved while the rider is operating within.

For example, my invention comprehends rotating it about its own axis or shifting its axis either with or without rotating it about its own axis and combining it with other features and devices calculated to add to the amusement effect of the whole.

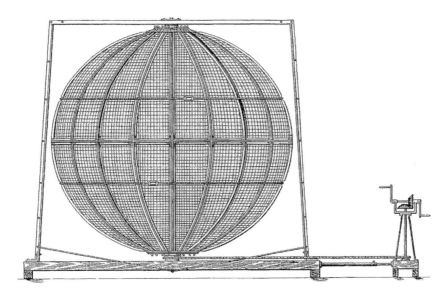

Depending within the whirl is a curtain of suitably-colored material, adapted to be connected with the rider's machine or otherwise operated in connection therewith, so that during the performance it will follow the performer in his circles within the whirl, swinging outwardly by centrifugal action as it is carried around inside and giving a peculiar, preferably generally colored or decorative, effect to the scene, it presenting a moving color scheme following or in conjunction with the operator. This constitutes one form of what, for want of a better term, I call a "mystifying" device, meaning by this a device which contained within the whirl is operated or moved by or in connection with the performer or presented in connection with him in such a manner as to mystify the scene and render it more perplexing to the onlooker that it would otherwise appear."

7. RECREATION

FAMILIAR SIGHT ON THE STREETS OF BUFFALO.

Lincoln County Leader, July 22, 1897
Toledo, Oregon

Light upon the pedal,
    Firm upon the seat,
Fortune's wheel in fetters
    Firm beneath our feet.
Leave the clouds behind us,
    Split the wind we meet,
Swift, oh, swift and silent
    Rolling down the street!

Bicycle Song
Harriet Prescott Spofford

A RIDE A DAY KEEPS THE DOCTOR AWAY

Buy a bike and ride to work in the fresh, clear morning air. Obviate all vexatious delays by riding your own bike. Be able to go where you want to when you want to. A "bike" in the family is Better Than The "Family Doctor" and far cheaper. Of course you will want a

IVER JOHNSON

Every Thing
For The Bicycle **KING BROTHERS** 110 East
Adams Street

Arizona Republican, May 05, 1919
Phoenix, Arizona

"I have invented certain new and useful Improvements in

Camera-Carriers for Bicycles.

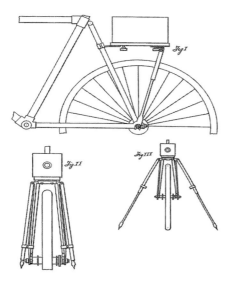

A great number of riders of bicycles are amateur photogra-
phers and when out on the road are desirous of taking "snap-
shots" at some striking scenery or other object of interest
which may present itself. The great drawback to this is the
inconvenience of carrying a camera and setting it up properly
when the occasion is presented.

(My invention) meets this inconvenience and provides a simple and cheap arrangement for carrying and supporting the
camera and setting it up at any point on the road."

United States Patent 0665480
Inventor: SOFTLEY EDWIN W (US)
Application Number: US1898665332A
Filing Date: January 3, 1898

"This invention relates especially to a means for supporting varying sizes of wire carrying **baskets from the bars of bicycles** and has for an object to produce a strong, rigid and easily mounted support which utilizes one or more clamping screws with which the usual handle bar post is equipped, as a means of securing the support without alternation of the bicycle equipment.

A still further object attained is to provide adjustment whereby means of **slots and bolts** through the supporting element and holes to receive the bolts through the strap of the basket a small basket may be substituted for a medium or larger size wire basket without changing the supporting element."

"The present invention has for an object to provide a **bag** characterized by its adaptability to a **wide variety of uses** and which may be supported or carried in any of a number of positions with full assurance that the contents will not slip out of the opening through which they were introduced while the bag is being carried. For example, a bag may be suspended from the shoulder and lie in a horizontal position as carried. It may similarly be supported on the handles of a bicycle or it may be carried on the back, and all while permitting the owner to use one or both hands for other purposes.

Another object of the invention is to provide a bag adapted to be suspended from the shoulder or any other suitable support by means of a rope or strap that also acts as a drawstring to open and close one end of the bag at will.

A still further object of the invention resides in an open-ended shoulder bag of such construction that the open end thereof automatically closes when the bag and its contents are picked up by the shoulder strap or are supported. by the shoulder strap.

A still further object of the invention resides in a bag of the type above described which is composed of a **light, strong material** which can be folded or rolled into a very small, compact condition when empty and not in use."

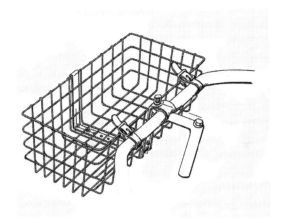

Inventor: Pawsat, Ewald F.
Application Number:
US52435131A
Publication Date: May 9, 1933

Inventors Molinari Jeanne
Publication number
US2552443 A
Publication type Grant
Publication date May 8, 1951

The value of bicycles in warfare has been fully demonstrated, and all the large armies of the world now have a bicycle corps. To meet the peculiar requirements of the case, however, special "military" bicycles are necessary, which differ from the ordinary type as much as the original high wheels differed from the modern racer. A military bicycle must have provisions for carrying the soldier's knapsack, canteen and gun, and the latter must be carried in a convenient position, so that the rider on jumping off may grasp it instantly.

Pullman Herald, Pullman, W.T. September 15, 1900

"The present invention relates generally to bicycles and more particularly to gun holders secured to bicycles.

One of the basic deficiencies in traveling by bicycle is the difficulty in carrying articles, especially elongated articles such as rifles. In addition to the problem of supporting the rifle while riding a bicycle, which normally requires the use of both hands, the danger of accidental discharge of the weapon is an important factor to be considered.

The present invention is concerned with a device which allows a bicycle rider to conveniently and safely carry a rifle along with him. This device consists essentially of an elongated scabbard, boot or holder secured in a substantially upright position on either the front or rear axle and fender out of the way of the rider.

The device is easily adapted to be formed economically out of a wide range of materials, for example the device could be formed from cardboard to carry a toy rifle or BB gun on a child's bicycle, or the device could be formed of heavy plastic or leather for use on either a regular bicycle or a motorized bicycle by either hunters or law enforcement officers."

United States Patent: 3142424
Inventor: Reed Jr., James R.
Application Number: US16983662A
Publication Date: 07/28/1964

Miss Dorothy Becker Riding a Surf Board at Honolulu, a Feat Rarely Accomplished by Any Except Native Kanakas.

The Day Book, Chicago, Ill. April 14, 1915

82

"**This** invention relates to carrying racks for vehicles and more specifically to a carrying rack structured for attachment to one side of a two-wheel vehicle for the purpose of mounting a surfboard aligned substantially in a vertical plane and parallel with the vehicle centerline axis.

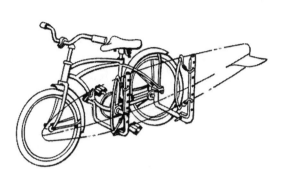

When a surfing enthusiast attempts to haul his surfboard by bicycle it is both a frustrating and dangerous endeavor. When the surfer wraps his arm around the center of the surfboard in an effort to firmly grasp the surfboard while attempting to steer the vehicle with only one hand, the surfboard oscillates up and down as the surfer peddles the bicycle and it becomes unavoidably very difficult to hold. The surfer

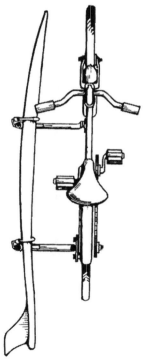

soon becomes weary from the physical strain of trying to both manually hold and transport the surfboard and this may result in impaired maneuverability and be a significant contributing factor in causing an accident that otherwise could be avoided.

For this type of rack the surfboard is secured above the bicycle and aligned in a horizontal plane which results in clearance problems for persons of different height and also presents the risk of the surfboard acting as an air foil at which time it becomes a safety hazard. If the surfboard is unsatisfactorily secured to the carrier rack or a primary securement component is defective and the surfboard topples it will invariably strike and possible seriously injure the person."

United States Patent 3659761
Inventor: WESSON, BOBBY DEAN
Application Number: 05/079723
Publication Date: 05/02/1972

"The present invention relates to carriers adapted to be mounted on bicycles and related vehicles, and more particularly refers to such carriers particularly adapted for supporting baseball bats and baseballs.

Baseball has become a **favorite national sport** and pastime for both young and old. It has become particularly popular among young people, witness the tremendous increase in the growing popularity of young people's baseball leagues such as Little League, Junior League, Pony League, etc. Because the playing fields are generally located at a considerable distance from the homes of the young players, the players almost invariably utilize bicycles for transportation to the playing field.

As anyone who has ridden a bicycle knows, it is extremely difficult and even **dangerous** to ride a bicycle while trying to hold a baseball bat in one hand.

For greatest safety, it is generally required that the bicycle rider use both hands to manipulate the bicycle. Riding while utilizing one hand to hold a bat is extremely dangerous and is responsible for numerous accidents. Moreover, there is a real danger that the baseball bat may get caught in the wheel spokes, resulting in the rider's being **thrown off** the bicycle. Standard carriers are sometimes utilized, but there is a tendency for the bat to bounce around and even bounce out of the carrier.

It is accordingly an object of the present invention to provide a devwwice which may be mounted on the frame of a bicycle for carrying a baseball bat.   It is a further object to provide such a device which **secures** the baseball bat so that it cannot be thrown off by the up and down motions of the bicycle.

It is still an additional object to provide a carrier device into which a baseball bat may be readily placed.   It is another object to provide a carrier device which prevents the baseball bat from interfering with the operation of the bicycle.

It is another object to provide a carrier mounted on the bicycle for holding a baseball securely, and for permitting instant removal therefrom.   It is still another object to provide carriers of the type described which are relatively **simple** to produce and relatively **inexpensive**."

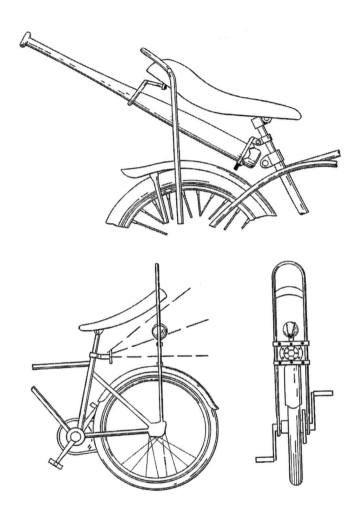

United States Patent 3907183
Inventor: Shearer Sr., David
Application Number: 05/387180
Publication Date: 09/23/1975

We should watch so carefully how far we allow ourselves to go in relaxing the rule of Sunday observance. The danger is that the habit grows stronger or weaker as we cultivate or neglect it. Begin to grow careless and you can never tell where you will end.

One does not need to be a Puritan to recognize the great moral and religious decadence which threatens our communities.

Our country homes, with the "week-end" house parties, have had not a little to do in starting this growing habit of indifference. First, the bicycle, then golf and the automobile have played their part. Beloved, let us do what lies in our power to keep alive in our own hearts and to rekindle in others the principle so beautifully set forth in the words of the Psalmist which we have chosen as our text, "O come let us worship and fall down, let us kneel before the Lord, our Maker." - Dean Craig.

The Presbyterian of the South, Atlanta, GA. March 2, 1910

"I claim:

A bicycle rack for supporting a golf bag on a bicycle having a collar clamp mounted around the seat post, a horizontal bag support extending rearwardly from the rear axle of the bicycle with slots at one end adapted to attach to the bicycle near the rear axle thereof,

an inclined bag support extending upwardly from the rear of said horizontal bag support, at least one seat brace between the seat post collar clamp and said inclined bag support,

at least one inclined support bracket between the seat post collar clamp and said horizontal bag support, wand means for connecting said inclined support bracket and said seat brace to said collar clamp,

said horizontal bag support and said inclined bag support being generally "U" shaped with two elongated branches and including portions at the "U" end that are inclined from the plane formed by said elongated branches to support the golf bag, the inclined portion of said horizontal bag support being inclined upwardly and supporting the bottom of the golf bag and tilting the golf bag toward the bicycle, the inclined portion of said inclined bag support being inclined inwardly toward the bicycle and supporting the golf bag near its top."

United States Patent 3827613
Inventor: MEYER M
Application Number: 05/305117
Publication Date: 08/06/1974

87

Herald and News., June 09, 1898
West Randolph, Vt.

"This invention relates generally to golfing accessories, and more particularly, to a golf club carrier for use on bicycles.

The golfer playing an average nine or eighteen hole golf course must cover a substantial distance carrying a heavy bag of numerous irons and woods used in playing the course. The golfer may walk the course carrying the bag on his shoulder, or may pull it behind in a small cart. If he chooses not to derive the benefits of the exercise inherent in walking, he may ride in a motorized or self propelled golf cart.

Pedal powered vehicles, such as bicycles and tricycles, have been devised to carry the golf bag. These rider propelled vehicles are more comfortable than walking and offer superior exercise. Some of these vehicles have expensive modified frames to receive the generally cylindrical golf bag. Others have a bag carrying frame adapted to be mounted on the vehicle.

The mounting of a generally cylindrical golf bag on such vehicles is not particularly desirable because the weight of the bag when full of clubs is difficult to balance. The size and shape of the golf bag is an impediment to securing the bag in a readily useful position. The mounting arrangement must not interfere with the normal operation of the vehicle and movements of the rider.

A further object of this invention is to provide a golf club carrier which when installed on bicycles provides the golfer with the benefits of cardiovascular stimulation, aerobic exercise, muscular development, and increased stamina while participating in his or her favorite sport."

United States Patent 4770326
Inventor: Thompson, Clifford A.   Publication Date: 09/1/1988

Suit to Suit Everything

A young fella noted for his eccentric habits possessed suits for every sport – cycling, fishing and everything else. Once day he was out fishing with his friend when the friend saw a fish rise.

"Cast there," said the friend. "It's a keeper!"

The youth looked at river, but never raised his rod.

"Why didn't you cast?" queried the friend.

"Well, I couldn't. I'm in my bicycle costume."

The Day Book, Octrober 1, 1912

"This invention relates primarily to bicycle fishing equipment carriers. With the onset of energy shortages and the popular reaction thereto by seeking means of transportation, wherever possible, alternative to a motor vehicle, it has been increasingly important to adapt bicycles for various carrying functions. For instance, a large segment of the population is involved in the sport or necessity of fishing.

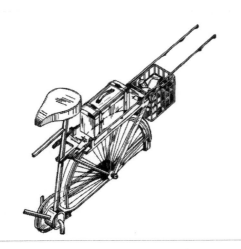

Fishing requires at the very least a fishing pole and usually a box (tackle box) used to contain fishing tackle, bait and hopefully the catch.

Presently available bicycle racks are disadvantageous for carrying fishing equipment since the available bicycle racks are usually too narrow transversely to fixedly support a tackle box and do not lend themselves easily to the attachment of fishing poles.

Furthermore, attempts have been made to provide a construction for a bicycle or a bicycle rack which enables the support of fishing poles in a generally vertical orientation. Such attempts have suffered the drawbacks of extending the fishing poles to a height which causes interference by trees and other overhangings with the smooth operation of a bicycle. Those attempts that have involved the horizontal orientation of a bicycle usually attached the fishing poles forward of the seat support such that the fishing poles, when attached to the bicycle, interfered with the operators legs and otherwise interfered with the proper operation of the bicycle.

Accordingly, a primary object of the present invention is to provide a bicycle rack suitable for carrying fishing equipment."

Publication number   US3921868 A
Publication date   Nov 25, 1975
Inventor Hyman Reichbach

8. TRAINING

There comes for the uses of the indoor rider little bicycle stands, trainers they are called, that will permit of riding in one's room. The bicycle is held stationary and slightly lifted from the floor.

One can regulate the amount of power required to push the pedals and if "hill climbing" is desired the thing can be tightened, or one can run on the level, if one pleases.

There are many kinds of home trainers and one can take one's choice of them.

The St. Louis Republic
June 08, 1902

Indoor Cyclist No Longer Simply An Ornament

An ancient proverb very wisely recommends us to combine the useful with the agreeable. The invention of indoor training machines for cyclists permits of putting this proposition in practice in the happiest manner. For some time the question has been put whether in-door bicycle training can be made to benefit to anybody? This is evidently what was asked by the author of the device shown in our engraving, and who, with much intelligence and very appositely, has discovered a pratical process of preventing a very appreciable source of energy from remaining unemployed.

In his system, the driving wheel, instead of revolving idly, is connected by an endless cord with the flywheel of a sewing machine or any other small apparatus that requies a moderate force to set it in motion.

PUTTING THE BICYCLE TO PRACTICAL USE.

Owing to this arrangement, each kick of the pedal is utilized, and the cyclist experiences the sweet satisfaction of knowing that while training himself in view of a coming race, he is also doing something useful. As may be seen, nothing could be better. But who would ever have expected to see the bicycle thus converted into an apparatus of domestic and practical utility.

Juniata Sentinel and Republican, February 06, 1895
Mifflintown, Pa.

"This invention relates to an improvement in training machines; and it consists in the peculiar construction and arrangement of the same, whereby the power and resistance are increased in direct proportion to the speed.

This machine is especially intended for use by bicycle-riders, and particularly such as desire to keep themselves in proper training while not enabled to use the bicycle by stress of weather or other causes.

The rider of this machine mounts it in the manner common to bicycles, and drives the large wheel with his feet, thereby revolving the fan-blades, which serve as a governor. In the use of the bicycle the resistance and consequent power increase directly with the speed, and this is a feature hitherto not obtained automatically in training-machines.

In the present device the increased speed of the fans creates an increased resistance to the air in direct and exact ratio to the speed, and the effect upon the rider is therefore precisely what would result from a similar use of the bicycle under the same conditions, and is perfectly automatic and needs no attention on the part of the rider."

Veröffentlichungsnummer   US351311 A
Publikationstyp   Erteilung
Veröffentlichungsdatum   19. Okt. 1886

Bicycle Home Trainer

A Michigan bicycle dealer has invented a home trainer and
exerciser that possesses many advantages. The inventor claims
that it gives all the exercise to hands, arms, legs and eyes
that riding on the road offers. There is the same necessity to
maintain a balance and, with the eyes closed, it is possible to
imagine youself gliding over smooth asphalt. The apparatue is
about two feet wide and five feet long, and weighs about fifty
pounds. Mr. Sturgis claims that this will be useful in bicycle
schools, and will save the teacher many weary miles of walking
and running after an erratic wheel as it wabbles along. The
beginner can fall off the home trainer as well as from a a wheel
or a track.

The Worthington Advance, Worthinton, Minn.
January 7, 1897

"**This** invention relates to that class of devices known in the art as **bicycle training** machines, which are provided to aid the novice in speedily attaining that degree of confidence in his ability to preserve his equilibrium while mounted on a bicycle necessary to enable him to ride unaided and with comparative safety.

In the view shown I have represented an ordinary bicycle of the safety type with **diamond frame** in elevation and represented the relative position of the parts of my invention.

[A]s the rider operates the pedals the motion of the rear wheel causes the belt to travel over the drums and impart motion to the front wheel, while the action of the suspended weights upholds the rider. The stops permit the tilting of the machine only within certain limits, which can be regulated by their adjustable nature. It is further evident that were some external power directed to one of the drums and the belt caused to travel the rider could then remove his feet from the pedals and devote his entire attention to guiding and preserving the equilibrium of the machine."

Veröffentlichungsnummer US604200 A
Publikationstyp   Erteilung
Veröffentlichungsdatum   17. Mai 1898
Eingetragen   12. Mai 1896
Erfinder Henry Vogeler

James Michael is the champion long distance bicyclist of the world. He recommends all wheelmen to take Paine's celery compound.

His experience is that of thousands of others. With the opening of the bicycle season many a young person and hundreds of older people who have determined to take up bicycling as a health-giving exercise find themselves really lacking the proper "snap" or stamina to begin on. Their bodily condition prevents so spirited exercise. They would like to ride, but they are out of sorts, run down by a winter of work or indoor life. Many who are really sick, who have sufffered from debility or wasting diseases for a long time until they have begun to think their troubles had become chronic, as nothing would give them relief. But this spendid exercise, like any other, requires strength to undertake. The blood is out of order, the nerves damaged, and natures's food for both is needed.

All such persons will find to their immense joy that Paine's celery compound, taken now, will make them well.

Paine's celery compound works wonders in the spring. If you have labored under the load of repeated headaches, neuralgic pains and days of nervous debility, now is your best time to get well.

The Butte Intermountain, May 16, 1901

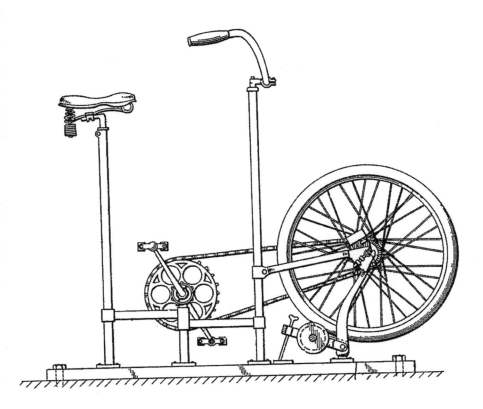

"**My** invention relates to stationary exercising apparatus patterned after the common form of bicycle, permitting the person using theh appartus to exercise the same muscles as in the case of riding a bicycle.

One of my objects is to provide in connection with the exercising apparatus, and observable to the one exercising thereon, indicating means which preferably indicate not only the speed at which the rider would be traveling if the apparatus were a bicycle, but also the mileage which he would cover.

Another object is to provide a neat, attractive, and economical construction of exercising apparatus of the general character above referred to."

Publication number   US1744607 A
Publication type   Grant
Publication date   Jan 21, 1930
Inventors   Baine James C

Wilbur Wright Leaves Quarter Million

Wilbut Wright, according to an accounting filed in the probate court, left an estimate of $279,296.40. The account was filed by Orville Wright, his brother, who gets the major part of the estate.

Twelve years ago Wilbur and Orville Wright were conducting a bicycle repair shop and were barely able to make ends meet.

The Seattle Post-Intelligencer, July 18, 1897

"**My** invention relates to **exercise apparatus** and more particularly to an exercise apparatus adapted to be used in connection with any standard make bicycle.

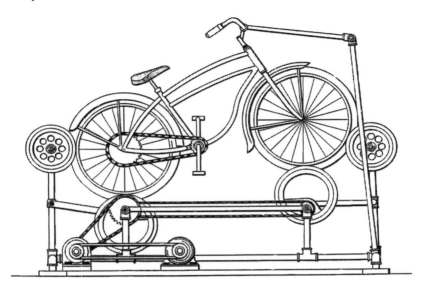

The object of my invention is to provide an exercising apparatus adapted to support a standard bicycle and to impart a swinging up and down movement to said bicycle.

A further object of my invention is to provide an apparatus equipped with two eccentrically supported rotatable wheels, each of which has a circumferential groove in its rim adapted to receive a portion of a corresponding bicycle tire therein and to engage the same frictionally, so that the bicycle wheel will be rotated, when the eccentric wheel is rotated or vice versa.

Another object of my invention is to provide an apparatus of the character indicated above making possible the in-door use of a bicycle for exercising purposes."

Inventor: Myers, William S.
Application Number: US78078247A
Publication Date: February 21, 1950

I have said that the action of riding a bicycle is not unnatural. That is true. The only novelty is in the combination of different muscular exertions. Below the waist a bicycle rider is running and climbing; that is, his action is different from running on a level. With the muscles of the groin and abdomen he is dancing. With the back and arms he is lifting. When I say dancing, of course I refer to the action of balancing. But this does not mean, as some people very foolishly have said, that a rider has to exert any force to keep himself from falling. The laws of nature attend to that. A man on a moving bicycle will no more fall over than a hoop will if you roll it across the room. The balancing which he does is the balancing of force and the maintenance of equilibrium between the upper part of his body and the legs that are active on a moving support. The work for the muscles I have indicated is that of maintaining a proper pose. It should be done with small expenditure of force, but well and carefully done.

Valuable Rules for Professionals and Amateur in Recorfds or Health. By Champion Jimmy" Michael, the Welsh Wonder.

The San Francisco Call, July 17, 1898

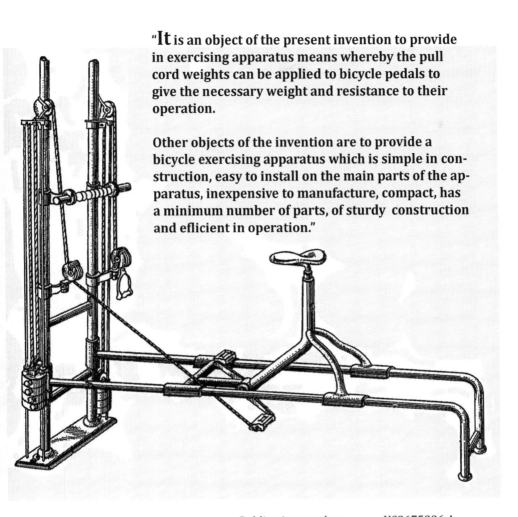

"It is an object of the present invention to provide in exercising apparatus means whereby the pull cord weights can be applied to bicycle pedals to give the necessary weight and resistance to their operation.

Other objects of the invention are to provide a bicycle exercising apparatus which is simple in construction, easy to install on the main parts of the apparatus, inexpensive to manufacture, compact, has a minimum number of parts, of sturdy construction and eflicient in operation."

Publication number   US2675236 A
Publication type   Grant
Publication date   Apr 13, 1954
Inventor   Harry Blickman

103

9. SCHWINN

Founded in 1895, the Arnold, Schwinn Company was once the largest single manufaturer of bicycles in the United States.

Frank W. Schwinn, son of founder Ignaz Schwinn, worked at the company from 1918 until his death in 1963. Known as a compulsive designer and drafterman, his name appears on 876 patents issued by the U.S. Patent and Trademark Office.

In 1950, the Schwinn Company's market share in the United States was 25 percent. However, by 1979 its presence in the US bicycle market had diminished to only 11 percent. The reason was a flood of imports and less expensive bicycles sold through big retailers and discount stores. At the time Schwinn remained committed to selling its more expensive bikes exclusively through a limited number of Schwinn dealers.

The Schwinn Company declared bankruptcy in 1992.

NOVEL BLACKLISTING CASE

The appellate court yesterday confirmed the lower court in a novel case, said to be the first of its kind in this country. Gustave-Horn won the suit. He sued the London Guarantee and Accident company for damages because the company had procured his discharge from the employ of Arnold Schwinn & Co, bicycle manufacturers. The insurance company insured the bicycle firm against injuries to its employees. Horn was hurt in the factory and he and the insurance company were unable to reach an agreement. It was then that the insurance people demanded and secured the discharge of Horn, threatening that unless he was let out it would cancel all of its insurance for the firm.

Rock Island Argus (Rock Island, Ill.)
March 7, 1902

BICYCLE BUSINESS BOOMING

The Proudfit Sporting Goods Co. have just unloaded a car of Arnold Schwinn Bicycles and two carloads of Iver Johnson, making three carloads, also a car of bicycle woodrims from the Tucker Woodrim Co. This makes the third carload of bicycles the Proudfit Sport Goods Co have unloaded since the first of the year. This is the largest shipment of bicycles made at one time in the western country.

The Ogden Standard (Ogden City, Utah)
February 5, 1915

"**My** invention relates more particularly to the handle bars of cycles.

One of my objects is to provide for the support of the handle bar in such 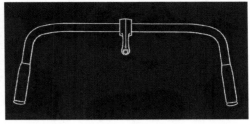 a way as to minimize the transmission of vibrations and shocks to the handle bar in the movement of the cycle over rough roads.

Another object is to provide a novel, simple and inexpensive construction for this purpose. Another object is to provide a handle bar and cushion assembly which will lend itself to adjustment in the clamping device of a handle-bar stem as in the case of handle bars as commonly provided."

United States Patent 2068474
Inventor: Schwinn, Frank W.
Application Number: US8299136A
Publication Date: 01/19/1937

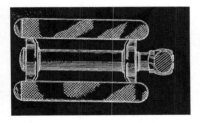 "**My** invention contemplates and provides certain improvements in pedals of the kind which are employed on bicycles, tricycles, etc.

A general object of my invention is to provide a pedal which is both light and strong and which is composed of elements that may be economically manufactured and easily and quickly assembled. Another object of my invention is to provide a pedal characterized by a novel and effective species of connection between its tread plates and suitable molded rubber covers or pads for such tread plates."

United States Patent 2178921
Inventor: Schwinn, Frank W.
Application Number: US19367638A
Publication Date: 11/07/1939

UNFAIR BICYCLE AND MOTORCYCLE MANUFACTURERS

Whereas, The Excelsior Motorcycle Company, manufacturers of the Excelsior and Henderson Motorcycle, and the Arnold Schwinn Bicycle Co., manufacturer of the World Bicycle, located in Chicago, Ill., ... have for the past nine months, and are at the present, waging a fight against organized labor. They have refused to grant the shorter workday and the union scale of wages and have secured an injunction which prohibits our members, or their friends and sympathizers, from in any way conducting peaceful picketing, or from telephoning, writing or speaking to any of the strike-breakers employed by these concerns.

Yours fraternally, FRANK MORRISON, Secretary, American Federation of Labor.

The Labor Journal, Everett, Wash.
January 14, 1921

"My invention contemplates and provides a bicycle frame of novel and graceful construction which is particularly well adapted to resist certain strains, resultant from accidental or other overloads, which frequently destroy ordinary bicycle frames,-i, e., those strains which tend to twist the axis of the steering head out of the plane which includes the axis of the saddle post mast, and those strains which tend to disrupt the union between the steering head and the reach tube which, in the normal use of the bicycle, constitutes a tension member acting between the steering head and the crank hanger.

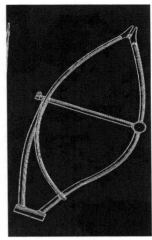

The primary object of the invention is to provide a bicycle frame of neat and sturdy appearance which is so constructed as to be well adapted to resist the destructive strains to which reference is made in the preceding paragraph. A secondary object is to provide a bicycle frame which, as an incident to its being greatly strengthened to resist the aforesaid strains, provides a natural pocket for a battery and/or tool box.

A salient feature of the frame of the present invention is that the upper stays of its rear wheel fork, after being welded to the upper portion of the saddle post mast, are extended and curved forwardly and downwardly in parallelism to the lower reach tube, and are welded to the latter,in such a way as effectively to resist those strains which tend to twist the axis of the steering head out of the plane of the axis of the saddle post mast.

Another important feature of the invention is that the lower reach tube, to which the extensions of the fork stays are welded as aforesaid, is slightly cambered so that it, and said stay extensions, yieldingly, rather than positively, resist strains which tend to tear the steering head away from the lower reach tube."

United States Patent 2151533
Inventor: Schwinn, Frank W.
Application Number: US19367738A
Publication Date: 3/21/1939

109

LOOKING AHEAD

In October 1944, 84 year-old Ignaz Schwinn, founder and acting president of Schwinn Bicyle Company, announced the donation of $25,000 to the Amateur Bicycle League of America. His intention was to promote amateur bike races with the hope that it would find a place in high school and college sports programs.

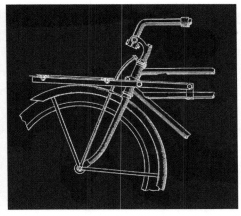

"**My** invention relates to bicycle carriers, and especially to package carriers mounted at the front end of a bicycle and supported directly on the frame, as distinguished from front carriers which are mounted on the front fork or handlebars.

One object of my invention is an improved mounting for such a carrier whereby the carrier is securely mounted on the frame by a cantilever arrangement, so that the weight of the load is carried primarily directly by the steering head and secondarily by an upward thrust on one of the rearwardly extending frame members.

Another object of my invention is a sturdy front carrier which may readily be attached to and detached from the bicycle frame and which, when detached, avoids any unsightly appearance of the bicycle. An alternative object is to provide a front carrier mounting which is more or less permanent,

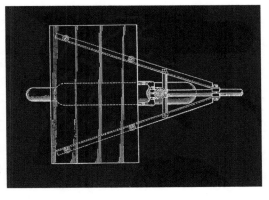

although it too may be detached for shipment in a flat bicycle crate."

United States Patent 2256629
Inventor: Schwinn, Frank W.
Application Number: US25973939A
Publication Date: 09/23/1941

112

"**My** invention relates to brake levers for bicycles and the like, and is particularly concerned with the mounting, upon a handle bar, of a brake lever which operates a Bowden wire, for example, to actuate a bicycle brake. I contemplate, however, that the lever and my mounting, whereby it is attached to a handle bar, may be employed for the control of speed changers as well as brakes.

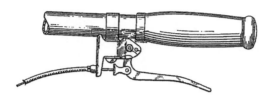

One object of my invention is a simplified and more economical mounting for the brake lever upon a handle bar, a mounting which is simple in construction and application, which holds the lever mounted in the desired position against slipping along or about the handle bar, and which, to a large extent, utilizes standard parts, such as standard nuts and bolts."

United States Patent 2237581
Inventor: Schwinn, Frank W.
Application Number: US32244240A
Publication Date: 04/08/1941

"The present invention relates to folding bicycle frames. One of the objects of the invention is the provision an improved joint for folding bicycle frames which is adapted to hold the parts of the frame with absolute rigidity when they are secured in the extended or operative position, and which is also adapted to be released with ease and readily moved to the folded position.

Another object of the invention is the provision of an improved folding bicycle frame, the parts of which are held in extended position with absolute rigidity, but which is adapted to be folded with a minimum amount of effort into a folded position where it occupies a minimum amount of space and where its projecting parts overlap each other.

Another object of the invention is the provision of an improved folding bicycle frame which is provided with a plurality of jointed sections adjacent its middle portion so that the front and rear wheels may be moved into a position adjacent each other and which is so arranged that they are held in this position by movable jointed members in readiness for quick movement to the operative position, where they may be secured with absolute rigidity.

Another object of the invention is the provision of an improved form of joint for folding bicycle frames, having a hinge to guide the folding movement, but in which all of the strain is removed from the hinge and taken by complementary. interlocking joint members, which may be secured together with absolute rigidity in operative position."

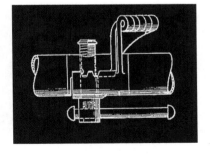

United States Patent 2372024
Inventor: Schwinn, Frank W.
Application Number: US49868643A
Publication Date: 03/20/1945

Made in the USA
Charleston, SC
12 November 2016